THE LITTLE BOOK OF
Big Corgi Butts

**Outrageously Cute Activities
to Celebrate the Greatest Booty on Earth**

• • • • • • • • • • • •

Zoey Acoff

Illustrated by Alexis Seabrook

Abrams Image | New York

CONTENTS

#1 Booty

CORGIS!

FOREWORD BY STEPHEN KING

My wife and I lived the first ten or twelve years of our marriage in a happily dogless state. Then one day my brother-in-law showed up with Jeremy, his corgi, and we fell in love. Didn't even need to talk about it; it was love at first sight. Since then we've always had a corgi or two to liven the place up, which they do just by being there. Right now it's two—Yoshi and Molly (aka the Thing of Evil). Before that there was Vixen, Frodo, Nixie, Marlowe, Juniper, and good old Bill, our first. None were pets. Each was a full-fledged member of the family.

Why corgis? Maybe because they would fit perfectly in the story of Goldilocks. Dig this: Corgis are not too big and not too small. Like Baby Bear's bed, corgis are just right. They're smart, they have a sense of humor (that fiendish corgi grin is a default position), and they're great watchdogs. No postman or FedEx driver goes undetected with a corgi in the house.

They enjoy toys, especially the ones that squeak, and if you can throw it, they will chase it. Every Frisbee is their friend. Corgis are just plain fun. You haven't really lived until you've watched a corgi locked and loaded, ready to snap any passing housefly out of the air (in our house we call such unfortunate insects "sky raisins"). Nor have you lived until you've seen a corgi after a big snowstorm. With their sturdy little legs, they go through snow like rowboats in a moderate chop.

They are smart, trainable, biddable, loving dogs. Best of all, though, are those butts. Take it from me, there's nothing in the canine world like a plump corgi backside. I've had people say, "Without a tail to wag, how do you know when he or she is happy?" Any corgi owner—we are a dedicated band of brothers and sisters—will tell you that you know, all right. You *absolutely* know. When you come home from a day trip, a week on the road, or just a jaunt to the supermarket, a corgi runs to you (and believe me, they run *fast*) with his or her entire rear end wagging joyfully back and forth. A corgi's butt is a corgi's joy-buzzer, and every time I see it, I fall in love again.

Corgis! Not too big and not too small.

Just right.

PREFACE

I was six when I saw my first corgi. My mom and I were at the airport, flying to LA to visit my grandmom, when I saw a chubby smudge of fur ahead of us on the moving walkway. I kept staring—what kind of dog has a heart-shaped bottom like that? Why is it so short? I could see it was wearing a red vest, with "DO NOT PET" on it in big block letters. I walked faster. The world around me disappeared. There was nothing but that floofy booty, bouncing hypnotically and only getting closer.

I bent down and stretched my hand out, knowing this would be the best pet—maybe the best moment—of my life. I reached, just inches between us, when suddenly my mom yelled, "Noooo!" She swatted my hand away and shuffled me off that walkway so fast I didn't even have time to whip out the tears.

I turned to look back at my missed connection, and he was giving me a woeful look, obviously as crushed as I was. We locked eyes. Time stopped. Life sparkled with meaning. Right then I knew that, one day, I would get my very own corgi. And I would pet it as much as I wanted to. And I would let everyone, everywhere, all across the world, pet it as much as they wanted to. We would be prancing unicorns of joy and glitter and soft tushies together, making the world a bouncier, fluffier place for all.

Fast forward to today, and I can definitely report that I am, in fact, a prancing unicorn of joy and glitter and soft tushies with Olive, my Pembroke. She is my light, my life, my everything. And yes, I do sit around and pet her all day. And yes, I do let anyone on the street pet her, and she loves every second of it. We're soulmates.

But what I've realized from the privilege—nay, the honor—of being mom to this rare and exquisite animal is that nearly everybody feels that spark of electricity when they lock eyes with her. People converge on her like she's a chubby magnet, and they melt into a puddle

of "oohs" and "awws" while I just sit back and mop it all up. Now I know that I definitely wasn't the first six-year-old to lose their scrunchie over a corgi, and every day I get to set the world right by bestowing all this doggie derrière on the next generation of six-year-olds.

It's my life's work.

That's why I could not be prouder of this book you're holding in your hands. *The Little Book of Big Corgi Butts* is the paean to the peachiest posterior that we all need. Packed with coloring pages, corgi facts, drawing prompts, crosswords, word searches, hard-hitting articles, and dozens of other activities, this is the book corgisessives all over the world have been waiting for.

So sit back, grab a pack of coloring pencils, a pencil, and an eraser, and get ready for a few blissful hours with the finest fanny on earth. Let the stressful and unimportant demands of life melt away as you learn dozens of corgi facts, color in sweet, sweet tushies, and up your intellect with corgi crosswords. You'll leave feeling replenished, re-centered, and reinvigorated to do what we were put on this earth to do: worship that booty.

—ZOEY ACOFF AND THE CORGIS ARE LIFE TEAM

• •

Zoey Acoff and the Corgis Are Life Team are a collaborative writing group that are totally real and entirely dedicated to the advancement of corgi art, science, and culture. They would like you to know that no corgis were harmed in the making of this book, but *maayybe* a few thousand treats were slipped to their muses, in the name of science.

DO YOU SPEAK CORGI?

THE DOXFORD

ENGLISH

DOGTIONARY

There is only one *Doxford English Dogtionary*. Renowned for its discerning discernment, delicious taste, and deep-seated ability to double as a booster seat for the shorties among us, the *Doxford English Dogtionary* is the guiding light in doggie discourse for the twenty-first century. Some call it gibberish; some call it slanguage; some call it exactly the puppy pillow talk you need to get that booty bouncing your way. Whatever you call it, every devotee of the derpiest dwarves in doggoland needs to know how to stump that walk and bork that talk.

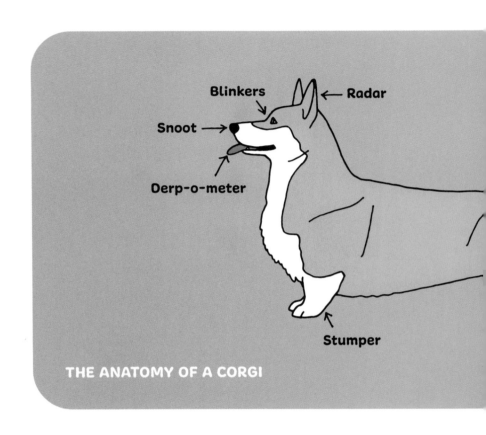

THE ANATOMY OF A CORGI

Blinkers

Radar

Snoot

Derp-o-meter

Stumper

Bork [boarck] verb / forms: borking, borked
to speak in dog
When a corgi wants to speak his mind, he'll keep borking until you've heard him.

Bean [bien] noun / plural: beans [bienz]
toe pads on the paw
The corgi pup ferociously flapped its paws and revealed the tiny beans on the bottom of each foot.

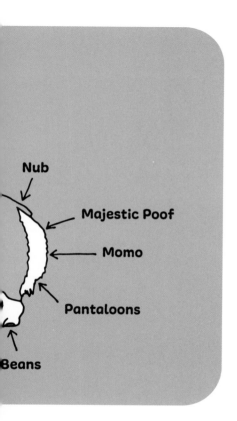

Nub

Majestic Poof

Momo

Pantaloons

Beans

Blep [blehp] verb / forms: blepping, blepped
sticking out the tip of the tongue and leaving it there
Exhausted from chasing bigger dogs with her little legs, Coco napped so hard that she blepped as she snoozed.

Blinker [bling-ker] noun / plural: blinkers [bling-kers]
a corgi eye
Rex couldn't take his blinkers off the red dot from the laser pointer.

Boop [boup] verb / forms: booping, booped
to gently bop something with a wet nose
Waffles stretched out her snout and booped Maggie in the forehead, then followed it up with a sloppy kiss.

Chonky [chahn-kee] adjective / superlative: chonkiest [chahn-kee-est]
the endearing quality of being a little chubby
For a petite pupper, corgis have big appetites and can easily get a little chonky.

Derp [durp] noun / plural: derps [durps]
silly corgi facial expression
Butters let his tongue loll out of his mouth and drip drool, his derp of the day.

Derp-o-meter [durp-oh-mee-ter] noun / plural: derp-o-meters [durp-oh-mee-terz]
the exposed section of a dog's tongue, which represents its degree of silliness
After excitedly chasing a squirrel, Rufus came back panting and displaying a maxed-out derp-o-meter.

Doggo [daw-goh] noun / plural: doggos [daw-gohz]

any good girl or good boy
A doggo is a gal's best friend.

FRAP [frapp] noun, verb / plural: FRAPs [frappz] / forms: FRAPing

Frantic Random Acts of Play, which are unique to corgis and often include sliding around on the floor
Every night before bedtime, Suzy gets a burst of energy and FRAPs around the kitchen island.

Floof [flewf] noun / plural: floofs [flewfs]

a very fluffy doggo or kitty
Although corgis have short fur, their fluffy butt makes them a definite floof.

Loaf [lohf] noun / plural: loaves [lohvz]

to form a bread-like shape
Charles, the red-headed corgi, tucked his paws under his body and went full-on loaf.

Majestic poof [muh-jeh-stick pouf] noun / plural: majestic poofs [muh-jeh-stick poufs]

an impressively fluffy corgi bottom
The second Matilda pranced on stage with her majestic poof, everyone knew she would steal first place in the corgi category.

Meerkat [mear-cat] verb / forms: meerkating, meerkated

to sit up on hind legs
To get a better view of the counter, the corgi meerkated and peered around.

Mlem [mlehm] noun / plural: mlems [mlehmz]

the sound of a doggo or cat lick
A doggo with a peanut-butter-covered nose goes "mlem."

Momo [mo-mo] noun / plural: momos [mo-moz]

Japanese for "peach," the slang term in Japanese for a corgi butt
Corduroy the corgi loves shaking his momo before finally settling down for a nap.

Nub [nuhb] noun / plural: nubs [nuhbz]

a short tail
You can count on a corgi to wag its nub wildly whenever you come back home.

Pantaloon [pan-tuh-loon] noun / plural: pantaloons [pan-tuh-loonz]

a section of longer hair around the hind legs, creating the appearance of wearing pants

We used a hair dryer after Missy's bath to fluff up her pantaloons to their max puff potential.

Peach [peech] noun / plural: peaches [pee-chez]

a corgi's butt; a fruit that best represents the shape of a corgi's behind

That corgi has the poofiest peach that has ever sat on a couch.

Pupper [puh-per] noun / plural: puppers [puh-perz]

a small, young, or adorable doggo

Barely six weeks old, Daisy is the most adorable corgi pupper I've ever seen.

Radar [ray-dar] noun / plural: radars [ray-darz]

the huge ears on top of a corgi's head

The pack of corgis all swiveled their radars at the sound of kibble falling in their bowls.

Snoot [snewt] noun / plural: snoots [snewts]

a nose, but cuter

As a short doggo, Max gets your attention by using his snoot to boop your ankle.

Sploot [splewt] verb / forms: splooting, splooted

to lie on the belly with hind legs splayed out on either side

On a hot day, corgis love to sploot on a cold floor and stretch out their stumpy legs to cool off.

Stumper [stuhm-per] noun / plural: stumpers [stuhm-pers]

short leg

Corgis' long bodies only make their stumpers look even shorter.

Woofer [wu-fur] noun / plural: woofers [wu-furs]

a very large dog, the opposite of a pupper but still charming

Next to her litter of tiny puppers, the proud corgi mom looked like a woofer.

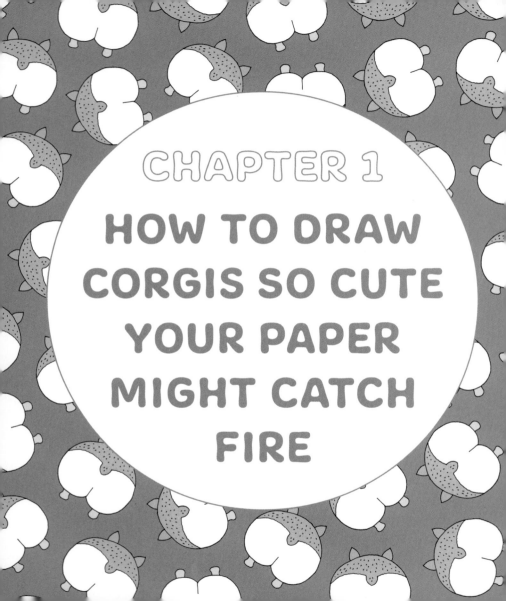

CHAPTER 1

HOW TO DRAW CORGIS SO CUTE YOUR PAPER MIGHT CATCH FIRE

HOW TO DRAW A SPLOOTING CORGI

Yes, every work memo from now on will need a splooting corgi doodled on it. Your coworkers will thank you, and your boss will see that you are, in fact, ready for a leadership position. (Don't know your sploot from your blep? Learn to speak corgi on page 8.)

STEP 1

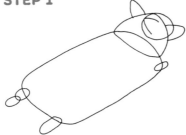

Roughly sketch large shapes for the corgi's head, ears, torso, legs, and feet. The shapes should overlap each other.

STEP 2

Erase the edges of the shapes that overlap the inside of the corgi's body. Add the shape of the tail and booty.

STEP 3

Start refining the outline of the corgi body around the butt, torso, legs, feet, and face. Erase and refine, working from the outside in. Make the booty outline more wiggly to add detail and interest.

STEP 4

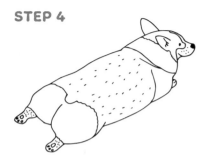

Finally, add all interior details such as the eye, nose, mouth, and beans on the paws, plus little short marks on the torso to show floof.

DRAW HERE

Your corgi is now full-sploot, and you can sit back and collect your raise, promotion, and gold watch for your service to humanity.

HOW TO DRAW
A DERPY CORGI

The derp-o-meter reports: Today will be sunny with a 110% chance of slobber on your favorite shoes. So grab a mop and a pencil, and let's draw this derpy doofus and his drool into existence.

STEP 1

Draw an oval face with two longer ovals at the top for ears. Add circles for the chest, body, and rump, then add smaller, longer ovals for his stumpers and feet.

STEP 2

Lightly sketch a vertical line from the top of the head to the halfway point of the oval. Lightly sketch a horizontal line two-thirds up the face oval (2). Add two shorter lines right below it (3, 4). Draw a smile at the bottom of this line. Add a small oval for a blep-y tongue.

STEP 3

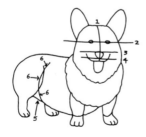

Smooth the transition between the back left leg and the tummy with a connecting line (5). Erase line 6. Add the eyes along line 2 and add the nose between lines 3 and 4. Erase the guidelines. Add chin hair detail by making the outline of the chin more jagged and wavy. Do the same with chest hair detail. Add two curved vertical lines to all four feet to show "toes." Refine the corgi's mouth so it appears less rounded, and add a small indentation under the nose.

STEP 4

Color in the nose and eyes, leaving small white circles in the upper left corners of both eyes as highlights. Add a short vertical line connecting the nose to the mouth in the center. Add scruff and dimension to the ears (see arrows 1 and 2). Add a vertical stripe that wraps around under corgi's eyes. (This would be a white marking in a color drawing.) Add a line on the back left leg to separate the foot from the leg (see arrow 5).

DRAW HERE

Mop up the slobber that your freshly sketched corgi just splattered all over your paper. But also, get used to it.

HOW TO DRAW
A UNICORGI
THAT LOVES YOU
VERY MUCH

We all need a friend. Sometimes those friends are imaginary. Sometimes they're mythical creatures. Sometimes we need to draw them for ourselves. Sometimes they're all three, and that's when they're the best friend we could ever ask for.

STEP 1

Break corgi down into large overlapping shapes as shown in the drawing, including the ears and the unicorn horn.

STEP 2

Erase overlapping lines inside the body and smooth transitions between the shapes.

STEP 3

Draw a vertical line parallel to the angle of the face from the center bottom of the unicorn horn to the chin cleft (1). Draw a curved horizontal line straight across near the base of the ears (2). Draw a second horizontal line straight across slightly above the bottom of the face (3).

STEP 4

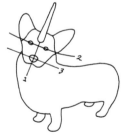

Position the eyes along line 2, and note that the outer corners of the eyes line up with the inner bottom corners of the ears. Position and center the nose where lines 1 and 3 intersect. Erase guidelines.

STEP 5

Color in the eyes and nose. Be sure to leave one small white circle in each eye as highlights. Add inside shapes to ears, face, and corgi's cardigan. Add two toe lines to each foot. Finally, add curved descending "candy cane" lines to the unicorn horn.

DRAW HERE

Your new BFF is ready for a lifetime of heart-to-hearts, sharing ice cream cones, and macraméing friendship bracelets with you. Hope you don't value your personal space!

HOW TO DRAW A LOAF OF BREAD THAT MIGHT ACTUALLY BE A CORGI

Look at that. Is it a loaf of bread? Or a corgi? Hard to tell from this angle. Hard to tell from all angles. Are we even sure there's a difference?

STEP 1

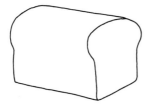

Draw an outline of the loaf of bread with the inside "slice" line, which also serves as the front of the loaf.

STEP 2

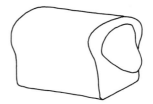

Add an outline of the corgi's face.

STEP 3

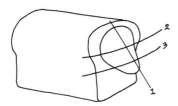

Draw a straight diagonal line two-thirds of the way over to the right side of the face (1). Next, draw a curved horizontal line about one-quarter of the way down from the top of the face (2). Now draw a second curved horizontal line two-thirds of the way down the face (3).

STEP 4

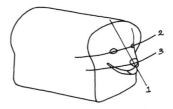

Erase the top outline of the face, leaving the sides and bottom. Add the eyes along line 2. Center the nose where lines 1 and 3 intersect. Add a derpy mouth. Note that the left corner of the mouth is the same height as the top of the nose. To create the top "lip," draw a curved line from the left side to just under the center of the nose. Add a smaller version of that line shape on the right side. Then draw the bottom "lip" following the original bottom line of the face. Add a tongue.

STEP 5

Erase the guidelines. Draw a stripe down the center of the forehead and nose. Curve the left side to the left so it's running parallel to the mouth with space in between. Keep the line wavy. Add little eyebrows. Color in the nose and eyes, leaving a small white circle in each eye as a highlight.

STEP 6

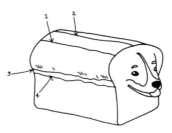

Draw two wavy lines parallel to the top of the loaf (arrows 1 and 2), then two wavy parallel lines under the top rounded "cap" of loaf (arrows 3 and 4). Add a few short diagonal texture lines just above them.

DRAW HERE

But, seriously, is it a loaf of bread or a corgi? You created it; you call it. We'll just be over here calling it THE BEST.

HOW TO DRAW A CHONKY FOOD THIEVIN' CORGI

Do *not* turn your back on that pizza. Ugh . . . too late. Chonkers the corgi stole a slice, and now he's giving you side eye because you should have just offered to share. He'll teach you some manners just as soon as he's done dripping grease all over his face, the rug, and your pillow.

STEP 1

Break corgi down into large, simple shapes as shown in the drawing. These can overlap.

STEP 2

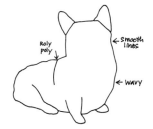

Erase overlapping lines inside the body. Erase the top lines of the legs. Make the outline wavy to show off the corgi's chonky body. Add a "roly poly" line starting from the mid back to almost the center of the body.

STEP 3

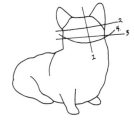

Draw a vertical line down the center of the face (1). Draw a horizontal line one-third of the way down the face, just under the ears (2). Draw a second horizontal line two-thirds of the way down the face (3). Draw an upward curving line under line 3, leaving a bit of space between them (4).

STEP 4

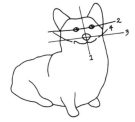

Position the eyes along line 2. Position the nose in the center where lines 1 and 3 intersect. Draw corgi's top "lip," starting as a curved line (aligned with the left edge of the left eye) and dipping down and back up into a point, then mirrored on the right side. Erase the guidelines.

STEP 5

To add the pizza, draw an inverted triangle with a line for the crust, circles for the pepperoni, and finger-like cheese shapes dripping off. Color in the nose and eyes, leaving a small white circle in each eye as a highlight and two small crescent moon shapes on the right sides. Add toe lines to each foot.

STEP 6

Add shapes inside the ears, a forehead stripe that widens around the snout, cardigan lines on the left and right, and an extra line on corgi's back leg (see arrows in drawing). Add small parallel lines inside the pepperoni slices.

DRAW HERE

If you want to put a stop to the side eye, draw eighteen thousand more slices of pizza. Chonky will let you know when he's had enough.

HOW TO DRAW THAT EMBARRASSING CORGI SELFIE THAT WON'T GO AWAY

You know that embarrassing double-chin selfie your corgi took? Now you can help him never live it down by drawing it on *everything*. You're just that kind of dog parent.

STEP 1

Draw a rough outline of the outer shape of corgi's head.

STEP 2

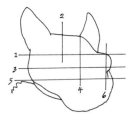

Draw the horizontal and vertical lines as shown.

STEP 3

Add the features. Position the eye in the center where lines 1 and 2 intersect. Draw the mouth between lines 4 and 6, and add the nose and right eye. The pointy top of corgi's mouth will start where lines 3 and 6 intersect. The bottom of the mouth will start where lines 5 and 6 intersect. The left side of corgi's mouth will start where lines 3 and 4 intersect. Erase the guidelines.

STEP 4

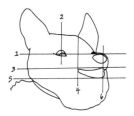

Add shapes inside the face: the white forehead stripe and area around the snout, the neck, and muzzle area, a bit of white above the top of the nose, the shapes inside the ears. Use your pencil to align the tops of shapes with other parts of the face.

STEP 5

Add more inside details: whisker dots, a dark thick outline inside the eye, collar hardware. Add a line inside the mouth to create a bottom "lip," curving it from the left corner of the mouth to the lower right side. Add teeth along the top of this line.

STEP 6

Color in the eye, leaving a small white circle in its upper left corner as the highlight. Also color in the nose.

STEP 7

Color in the inside of the mouth. Add small, horizontal parallel lines inside the shape next to the left eye. Then add the same parallel lines inside the lower lip and the shape between the nose and the mouth.

STEP 8

Finally, make the outer outline of corgi's fur fluffier and softer with small, pointy ridges close together. Add little short fur marks inside the ears and on the face. Add stitches to the collar.

DRAW HERE

Take a photo of the selfie (it's SO bad, lolol!) and post on the Internet, dog park bulletin board, and every highway billboard within a hundred miles. Have T-shirts made. Have hats made. And no, you don't need to get a life. Corgis *are* life.

HOW TO DRAW A CORGI STRIKING FOR BELLY RUBS

Belly rubs now! Belly rubs loud! Belly rubs proud! This corgi could use some work on his protest chants, but he'll always stand up for justice. And by that he means lie down for belly rubs. He insists it's the original sit-down strike.

STEP 1

Draw a rough outline of the outer shape of the upside-down corgi.

STEP 2

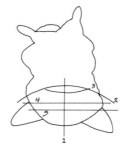

Add two connecting lines (a V-shape) to separate the tail from the body at the top. Add lines to separate the ears from the head, and then draw the lines numbered 1 to 5 as shown.

STEP 3

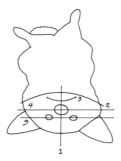

Add the eyes on the bottom horizontal line (5), equidistant from the vertical line. Center the nose where lines 1 and 4 intersect. Erase the sides of line 3 so you're left with just the mouth.

STEP 4

Add the front legs and paws. Erase the guidelines.

STEP 5

Add the inside shapes around the nose, mouth, and front right paw. Add more shapes inside the ears, draw a jagged line across the chest, and soften the outer outline.

STEP 6

Color in the nose and eyes. Leave a small white circle in the upper left corner of each iris as a highlight.

STEP 7

Add horizontal parallel lines inside the large shape around the mouth, and in the smaller shapes on either side of the mouth. Draw more fur lines in the chest area.

STEP 8

Add more fur lines all over the body from the tail to the face.

DRAW HERE

Give your brand-new activist some poster board, markers, and plenty of glitter so he can fight for his rights. He definitely won't roll all over it and glitter bomb your entire existence. Not a chance.

HOW TO DRAW A CORGI THAT'S ALREADY TOO COOL FOR YOU

Oh, you're into doodling? This corgi was into doodling before you ever picked up a pencil. And no, it doesn't matter that he didn't exist before you drew him.

STEP 1

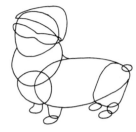

Draw a series of overlapping rounded shapes for the hat, head, upper and lower chest, torso, legs, feet, tail, and shades.

STEP 2

Refine the outline by smoothing and erasing overlapping lines inside the body. Make the hind leg outline wavy. Add a cleft to the chin.

STEP 3

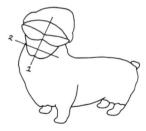

Draw a vertical line (1) through the center of the face. This line will be on an angle, parallel to the angle of the face. Draw a horizontal line three-quarters of the way down the head (2). Add a wavy vertical line to separate the front left leg from the torso.

STEP 4

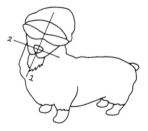

Center the nose where the two lines intersect and add a beard with jagged ends. Erase the guidelines.

STEP 5

Draw a wavy line from the back of corgi's neck (top arrow) to where the front left leg intersects with the chest (bottom arrow). Draw a stripe down the forehead and then add a curved line on either side of the nose to create the snout.

STEP 6

Draw an extra curved line one-third of the way up the beanie. Add curved vertical lines to show knitted ribs.

STEP 7

Draw short fur marks all over the torso and add toes to the feet by adding two curved lines.

STEP 8

Color in the nose. Add three horizontal lines to the glasses to create slatted shades.

DRAW HERE

"Can you back up, man? You have, like, zero chill," says your new ungrateful corgi friend. Do as he says. You'll only look even dorkier if you fight it.

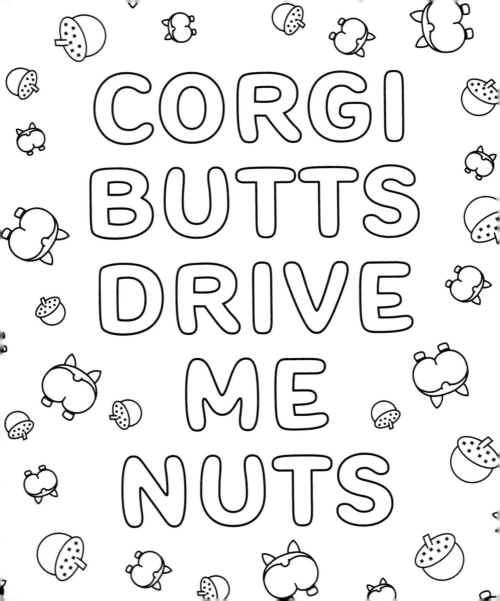

LIFE IS SHORT.
SO ARE MY LEGS.

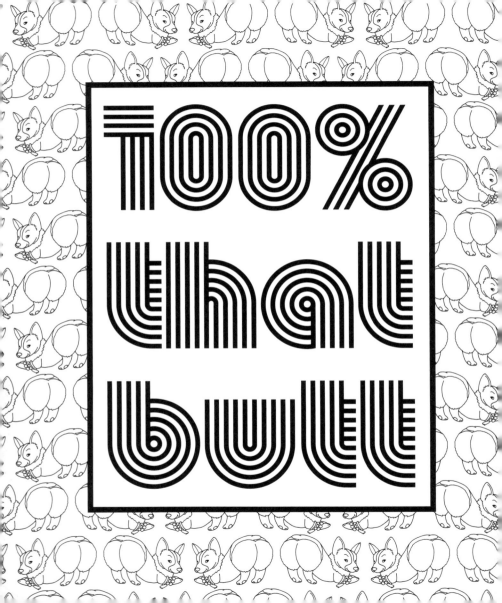

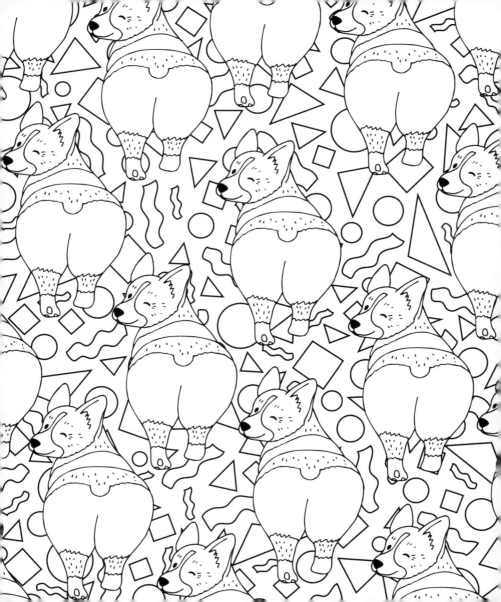

COFFEES

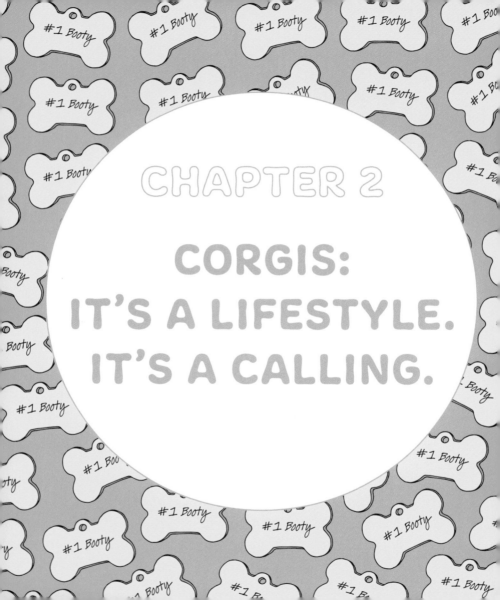

CHAPTER 2

CORGIS:
IT'S A LIFESTYLE.
IT'S A CALLING.

THE CORGI ACCESSORIES YOU ABSOLUTELY MUST HAVE

Yes, you want a corgi. Yes, I want a corgi. Yes, everyone on the planet wants a corgi because don't we want world peace? But if you're not ready for a full-time fluffer or if commitment, even to the sweetest soulmate, scares you, then you definitely need to dry your tears with some plastic shaped like a corgi.

We know you probably already have a corgi T-shirt, corgi socks, and a corgi mug, but do you have the corgi hat, phone case, tote bag, blanket, plush toy, stickers, bottle opener, scarf, throw pillow, and leggings with your own corgi butt on the butt? Have you invested yet in a booty-shaped headrest, a booty-shaped purse, and a booty-shaped toilet seat? If not, level up, loser! You can't join the coolest cult on the planet without spending every minute and dollar you have proving you fit in. Start with these five real-life corgo-replacers, and soon that bum-sized hole in your heart will be brimming with corgi clutter of the cutest conception.

CORGI HEATING PAD

If you can't have a warm corgi nestled next to you, radiating body heat and booping you now and then, get the next best thing: a corgi-shaped heating pad. We've seen it in both chonky sizes, like a puffo corgo you just want to squeezo (yes, we did), and in flat, fluffy big-booty sizes, perfect for draping on a sore shoulder or petting and talking to because, yes, she *is* a very good girl. These corgi heating pads are 100% guaranteed to melt your cold, hard heart no matter how many times people refused to talk about corgis that day.

CORGI PLANT HOLDER

Did you know that corgis have been clinically shown to reduce stress one thousand times better than plants? It's true—look it up. (Don't.) But thanks to the innovations of science, industry, and the wild place that is the Internet, you can now have the benefits of both with an almost-too-cute corgi plant holder. Available in standing, sitting, and splooting models, they go perfectly with any décor, can easily cover every open surface in your home, and will undoubtedly win you friends and lasting health and happiness. With a thousand or so of these in your house, you'll be well on your way to being the crazy corgi plant lady everyone already thinks you are.

CORGI ONESIE

Want to get ahead in life? Throw on this power suit next time you have an important meeting, big presentation, or chance to bark at your boss. Yes, it's technically marketed as a costume, but you're an outside-the-box thinker, and everyone at work should see what an innovator you are. You will also look SO cute. And everybody knows that cute is what gets the job done. Just be careful not to shake your felted fanny down the hall too much—Brad in accounting is already way too in love with you.

CORGI HOODIE

If corgis have taught us one thing it's that we need to lounge harder and work never. So go ahead and take this opportunity to quit your job (see to the left for your storming-out-the-door outfit) and use the last dregs of your bank account to buy this shockingly essential and floofy corgi hoodie. Dozens of styles are available online and in stores, making it the perfect wardrobe staple to replace all your other tops. It also comes with a built-in zen mindfulness retreat—just pull the handy cords on the hood tight, and ta-da, you're hidden from the world and its unreasonable, unenlightened demands. It's just you and your friend Corgi Hoodie from now on!

CORGI ARTWORK

Now that you are living your Very Extremely Best Life, you need just one last thing: *Welsh Corgi Riding a Narwhal*, the stunning portrait of one of the greatest sea-creature-riding corgis of all time. For under thirty dollars, you can be the owner of this original tea-stained print, created using antique scientific illustrations and possibly drugs. These popular artworks evoke ancient manuscripts, and the hand-painted tea-staining technique ensures that each piece is completely unique and soundly unregiftable. As one reviewer put it: "The look on my husband's face . . ." This peerless collectible is guaranteed to elicit all kinds of expressions, and you'll quickly find out who in your life lacks culture and refinement.

THIS CORGI KEYCHAIN WANTS TO BE EVERYWHERE WITH YOU STARTING NOW

The annoying thing about life is that you can't take a corgi with you everywhere you go. Even more devastating, there are only so many corgi socks, sweaters, leggings, scarves, and hats you can layer on before you lose the movement of your arms and legs. Luckily, we've spent days sobbing over this sorry state of things, and we have good news: you actually *can* take a corgi with you everywhere you go, if your corgi is also carrying your keys.

Even better, you can fit approximately twelve of these cute little guys on your key ring if you throw out your keys, and with a little hot glue and a magnet, this keychain also doubles as décor for your refrigerator, file cabinet, and car exterior. Do you want to celebrate any holiday known to humanity? This felted fluffer needs only a ribbon draped from his upper poof to deck your halls, festoon your turkey, or accent your diyas. And yes, it does also function as a good luck talisman when stuffed with corgi fur tumbleweeds. So let's get to it—if you start now, you'll have enough of these made by the time you make your first human friend.

• •

- **1 (8" × 12") white felt fabric sheet**
- **1 (8" × 12") tan or orange felt fabric sheet**
- Scissors
- **White thread**
- **Sewing needle**
- Hot glue gun
- **Small handful of craft stuffing, or corgi fur**
- **Fine-tipped black marker**
- **Black fabric paint (optional)**
- **Small paintbrush (optional)**
- **Keychain ring with chain**

1. Trace the corgi head template onto a white piece of felt. Repeat to make a second head, then cut them both out.

2. On the orange felt, trace the corgi eye patch template twice. Cut both out.

3. Take one of the white corgi heads and line up the orange eye patches so they're slanted along the top, with one of their long sides flush with the edge of the white felt.

4. Sew all around the eye patches to attach them. Then cut off the white ears, following the curve of the head.

5. Use the ear template to trace two triangles on the orange felt and cut them out.

6. Take the white felt head without eye patches and lay the orange triangles on top of the ears. Attach the triangles with hot glue.

7. Pick up the white felt with eye patches and lay it on top of the white felt with ears. All of the orange bits should be facing up.

8. Starting at the bottom, sew all around the head (follow the curve under the ears!), but stop sewing around the four o'clock position. Don't cut the thread.

9. You should have a gap near the bottom. Through this, add stuffing until it's plush, then sew the gap closed.

10. Now your friend needs a face. Using a black marker or fabric paint and brush, add two round eyes on the eye patches. Add a smaller oval nose in the middle of the white snoot blaze. Draw a teeny little smile below the nose.

11. Once everything is dry, sew the bottom ring of a keychain loop to the top of the corgi's head.

YOU'RE DONE!
And your new buddy told me to tell you: Thanks for being a friend.

CRUSH YOUR FRIENDS AT CORGI TRIVIA

Here's some simple math: there is a finite number of corgis on this planet at any one time. Yet there are hundreds, if not thousands, of humans on the planet. So according to our calculations, there are not enough corgis per capita. This means our only hope of securing maximum corg is to launch a civil war against everyone around us and capture their corgis for our own use. A great way to do this under the guise of "fun" and "companionship" is by inviting your future enemies over for a night of trivia. Then, slowly, question by question, you will assert your dominance and prove, once and for all, that you are Master of the Corgiverse. They will be left with no choice but to hand over their corgis, and you will enter the higher realm of Corgivana at last.

STEP 1
INVITE YOUR FRIEND-LIKE HUMANS

The first step to making the world a better place just for you is to draw your competitors into your domain by extending a "friendly" invitation. Consider sending a tasteful text message with an appropriate number of exclamation points and emojis. In our experience, the more emojis, the more harmless people think you are. Call them your "friends," tell them you "miss them, it's been way too long!" but that "life has been so busy!!!" and you want to "get together for a fun trivia night at my place!" Remember to delete the quotation marks before copying and pasting this drivel to them—we've made *that* mistake before, lol! ☺☺

STEP 2
PROVIDE TREATS

Just like corgis, humans become slow and sleepy when given enough treats, so treats, and possibly alcohol, are going to be a big part of your winning strategy. On the day of your looming victory over the Corgiverse, buy the cheapest, crappiest snack foods, baked goods, and grain alcohol you can find, then invest a little time upfront in decorating them to look like corgis or pouring them into corgi-themed cups. This will lure your friends into thinking the snacks you've provided are delicious while also keeping you very repulsed by them. Let them chow down when they arrive, while you remain lithe, alert, and ready to annihilate.

STEP 3
IT'S FLEX TIME

The moment has finally arrived to show off your unparalleled grasp of the entire corgi cultural canon. Although you surely know everything there is to know about corgis, and heck, you're the one that came up with the questions, make sure you have a few back-pocket ways to cheat, just in case someone beats you to an answer. It may seem mean-spirited or wrong, but do it for the corgis. They need you.

THE CORGI TRIVIA QUESTION STARTER PACK

Kick things off with these easy trivia questions before diving deeper into the gold mines of corgi history with questions such as, "When was the last time I petted a corgi, and what was I wearing?" and "How much better of a corgi parent am I than you? It's a 100-part answer."

• •

1. Corgis are originally from _____, but according to local legend, these magical pups actually come from _____.

2. Name every breed of corgi.

3. Although corgis are famous for their looks, they have a lot of brains behind that beauty and rank as the _____ smartest doggo among all woofers.

4. The word "corgi" means "_____ _____" in Welsh.

5. True or false: All corgis have nubs for tails.

6. Corgis were bred to be expert what? (A) hunting dogs, (B) herd dogs, or (C) water dogs

7. The first Southern California Corgi Beach Day meet-up event happened in what year?

8. What two foods commonly represent the shape of a corgi's booty?

9. Despite their tiny stumpers, corgis can run twice as fast as _____.

10. Pembroke Welsh corgis can come in five distinct colors, which are _____, _____, _____, _____, and _____.

11. The corgi's closet doggo relative is what? (A) Shiba Inu, (B) rat terrier, (C) Siberian husky

12. True or false: Long-haired corgis exist.

13. A Chigi is a mix between a corgi and a _____.

14. Who was the British monarch that made the Pembroke Welsh corgi synonymous with the crown?

15. The Cardigan Welsh corgi and the Pembroke Welsh corgi were officially recognized as two distinct breeds of corgi in what year?

ANSWERS ON PAGE 204!

CORGI BUTTS MAKE THE BEST BOOKMARKS AND BIRTHDAY CARDS

What's better than dog-earing your page? Corgi-butting your page. And what's better than a birthday? A birthday that includes getting down with some corgi booty. Now you can do both while also having a very cutesy crafty afternoon all to yourself.

For the bookmarks: If you are That Kind of Person and have a laminating machine, laminate the bookmarks to preserve them for posterity. If you are lazy and not crafty (hi, we love you), use clear packing tape to wrap each side of your bookmark and trim the edges. Try not to smirk every time you tuck your buttmark into the spine of this book, now your only acceptable reading material.

For the birthday card: Color it in to your heart's content, pour out your heart in a sweet message, then hand-deliver while making big heart-eyes at your friend. You've now made a friend for eternity, and yes, we know you gave it to the corgi up the street.

If you have a library
& a corgi you have
everything you need.

This is my corgi buttmark.

Any questions?

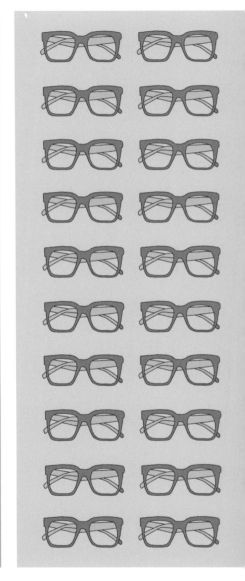

GO SHORTY IT'S YOUR BIRTHDAY.

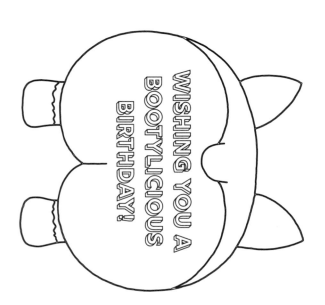

WISHING YOU A BOOTYLICIOUS BIRTHDAY!

CORGI CUPCAKES SO CUTE YOUR HEAD MIGHT EXPLODE

After extensive research, our team of corgi scientists have found that there are only two things on earth cuter than corgis: cupcakes, and kittens riding corgis like little ponies. We scoured the earth, and that was it. And because our jobs are to pummel you with cute until your head explodes, we decided to leave this corgi cupcake recipe here *juusstt* to see what happened.

This recipe will give you a moist, soft, sweet vanilla cupcake—it's the cupcake equivalent of getting the gentlest boop and cuddle from a sleepy corgi. Once you've mastered this little delight, you can experiment with other flavors and toppings, like red velvet or salted caramel. (Corgis love salted caramel, another surprising finding from our fake study.) Maybe your pupper cupper has a chocolate bottom and a vanilla top? Maybe she's blue merle with a cookie dough collar?

And because we know you have some blazing hot takes on the Pembroke vs. Cardigan question, we'll show you exactly how to decorate both, so you can battle your cupcakes to the cutest death. And if you want to sculpt tiny kittens riding your tiny corgi out of frosting, well, the universe exploding will be worth it.

Makes 12 cupcakes

FOR THE CUPCAKES:

1⅓ cups all-purpose flour

1¼ teaspoons baking powder

½ teaspoon salt

½ cup (1 stick) unsalted butter, softened

1 cup granulated sugar

2 large eggs

2 teaspoons vanilla extract

½ cup sour cream

FOR THE FROSTING:

8 ounces cream cheese, softened

½ cup (1 stick) unsalted butter, softened

1 teaspoon vanilla extract

⅛ teaspoon salt

3 cups confectioners' sugar

TO DECORATE:

Red and yellow food coloring (for Pembrokes)

Black food coloring

6 graham crackers

12 chocolate chips

24 mini chocolate chips

1. Preheat the oven to 350°F (180°C).

2. Line a muffin pan with paper liners.

3. Make the cupcakes: In a large bowl, mix the flour, baking powder, and salt.

4. In another large bowl, using a handheld or a stand mixer, beat the butter and sugar until fluffy. Add the eggs, one at a time, beating until incorporated, then add the vanilla and sour cream.

5. Slowly add the dry ingredients to the butter-sugar mixture and mix until just incorporated. Scoop the batter into the liners, filling each liner about two-thirds of the way up.

6. Bake for 18 to 22 minutes, until a toothpick inserted into the center comes out clean. Let cool on a rack before frosting.

7. While the cupcakes bake, make the frosting: Using a handheld or stand mixer, beat the cream cheese, butter, vanilla, and salt on low speed until combined. Increase the speed to medium-high and beat for about 2 minutes, until light and fluffy. Decrease the speed to low, then add 2 cups of the confectioners' sugar and beat until combined. Add the remaining 1 cup confectioners' sugar and beat.

8. Once all the confectioners' sugar is incorporated, increase the speed to medium-high and beat for 1 minute, or until light and fluffy.

9. Spoon ⅔ cup of the frosting into a small bowl. If making Cardigans, add 10 drops of black food coloring and mix until the color is even. If making Pembrokes, separate 2 tablespoons of the frosting into another small bowl. To the larger bowl, add 1 drop of red food coloring and 10 drops of yellow food coloring and mix until color is an even tan. To the smaller bowl, add 3 drops of black food coloring and mix until the color is even.

10. Decorate the cupcakes: Use a butter knife to smooth white frosting on each cupcake. Using a piping bag with a small tip, or a small spoon, carefully dab tan frosting for a Pembroke or black frosting for a Cardigan in two unconnected semicircles on each side, like the pattern on a tennis ball. The white frosting should peek out like a corgi's snout with a white blaze between its eyes.

11. Place one chocolate chip on the white snout as a nose and two mini chocolate chips on the face as eyes. To add a mouth, carefully pipe a curved line below the nose with the black frosting. For a Pembroke, cut a graham cracker into two small triangles and stick them into the frosting at either side of the head as ears. For a Cardigan, cut a graham cracker into two larger rounded triangles and stick into the frosting as ears.

YOU'RE DONE—time to gobble up these sweet little goobers!

feelin'
on top of
the world

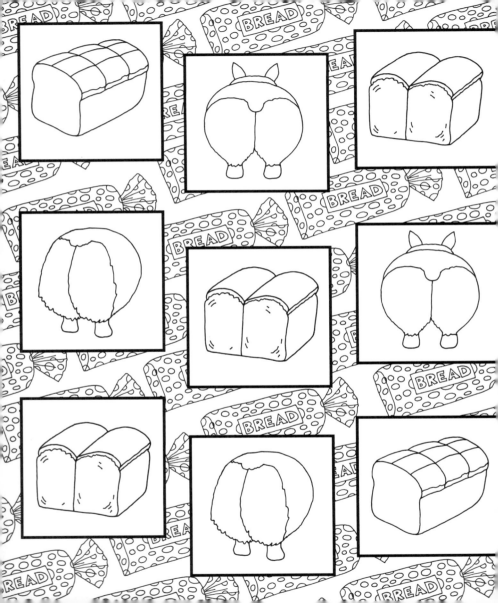

CHONKY CROSSWORDS + WOOFY WORD SEARCHES

A CHOWDOWN FOR CHONKERS

Chonkers the Corgi is STARVING. He's ready to eat the whole world and everything in it, but he'll also settle for chowing down on his twelve favorite foods. The only problem is: he can't find them in this word salad. And salad is *not* what Chonkers wants right now. Help a hungry doggo out and fetch his favorite foods from this extra-yummy word search.

```
B K L J T F T B W U M V N T X U J H C A L Y
Y F W W P S G A O B P U Y W L U V V B M Z P
C L S N O R A T N A P N S H W G X W V L H C
K F A Q J X C O D K D O K P H G B S A A F G
T A O G C O X T R O K Z X G F E P N S Y X B
S A H C O O P M O K H A Q R L N G L L R L H
E G V O B O K C U Y R X K S L V Q C F W Q A
D H E R I U D B S W C O M Q R U S G E K W A
J F U G B T K B L H B D B A N F O I Z W S T
Y R T S A P F O O P L Q D R M M E Z E L B J
L A Q I S W O N A I G R E P P U P K I N Z L
L P Q C Z V K O F L X E U H T P Z P G C R C
F P Y L Y U D M Y M O V M K F V Z M M U Y F
P Y Q E T Y B E D H K P Y S W I N Y J H M U
Z C G E I H V L B K V B C I G L F J J X U D
Q C R I A X C E Y O O P K I E I R M Z I V Y
D I O E U C F T R F F Y P N I R I N X Q R A
E N F M A S A Q F I B G G S J Y P T I C K Y
H O F H M F W E T Y I J V D Y B E A R X X D
O Y B F W Q E O G L Z N E I T J P Q J B Z I
C U L H G H H B K S P Q Q Q G P D G E P B A
S Y N G H M B H O V B R J N S T K Y Z H U C
```

CHONKUTERIE

CORGSICLE

LA GOOD BOIX

PUPKIN

FRAPPYCCINO

KOMPOOCHA

WONDROUS LOAF

PUPPERGIANO

POOF PASTRY

BORK ROAST

PANTARONS

NOMELET

HALLOWEEN 🌙
TREAT-OR-TREAT

It's Halloween, and the corgis are feeling extra cute. They're primping their pantaloons, floofing their floof, and doing tushie wiggles in the mirror, all so they can hit that sidewalk and nab those treats. But . . . they just can't decide what they want to be this year. Luckily, we hung an unbearably cute selection of costumes in our imaginary closet for them, and they just need to fashion show their way through them. So help them dig up and try on the costumes in this word search before they give up and go . . . butt naked.

```
L A T Q H X U H B Z X L R B I L R N
W I S O P A U D X V O J O U K O O S
X N T L T B I Z A A H O P C O W L H
M X T T G R F R L F T U I A T R I O
Y G K B L O E O Y Y F T R I S I A R
G W V E J E H T B P S N N N M D S T
V N V P N O S R A Y O Y S H S E Y Y
J K C W J H E T R T T O E R H R T B
R B J H M A B E M R H G P I U L O U
K P I A D B T Q E E I C V E N O O S
A G X L X T I X I G R M U U R B L K
R H O O U A K V X B C M N O X S P I
A A V B A X N A P X S C A T C T S P
F H O T T E R D O G G E R I K E V G
E N R U O B S O F Y Z Z U F D R O L
G R O C I N U D E G Z X D V F R M Z
M Y X L H J I H W Q W V V E I P D I
Q Q K U T X C I Q F N K T C N P M D
```

SHORTY BUS

COUCH TATER TOT

TINY T-REX

UNICORG

BUTTERY STICK

LITTLEST MERMAID

HAIRY POOPER

LOWRIDER LOBSTER

BOOTY BREAD LOAF

HOTTER DOGGER

SPLOOTY SAILOR

FUZZY FOSBOURNE

A VERY WEIRD DAY
IN THE LIFE
OF A CORGO

Corgis really, really like people. Which is adorable, because they're the only ones! In fact, if you own a corgi, it is probably standing right behind you at this moment, gazing lovingly at your back. Aww. When they're not staring at you, lying on your lap, or falling asleep on your face, they also love making up their own games. Especially if those games are inexplicable, like boinging the doorstopper or attacking rude toilet paper rolls. What are some other very weird things they like to do? Dig up these words that are all about what our not-at-all-elusive corgis are really up to when nobody's home.

```
S  U  F  E  F  D  Y  S  V  Y  G  U  G  G  Z  X  A  B  N  H  R  Q
D  H  A  R  Y  R  E  T  B  B  P  K  T  Z  H  D  G  N  B  E  Y  S
F  V  R  N  U  I  A  U  D  A  G  R  G  Q  X  S  O  R  P  C  P  N
N  V  T  E  M  R  T  P  T  A  C  Z  W  T  V  D  Y  A  J  I  C  R
D  D  L  O  D  T  J  C  N  V  A  E  C  Y  L  L  P  B  U  G  P  I
Y  D  O  C  S  C  J  B  A  Y  S  V  C  Q  I  K  A  W  O  Z  A  A
Z  Z  R  C  Q  J  O  H  T  P  H  P  U  A  C  T  N  H  L  A  W  L
O  B  O  Y  D  B  I  U  Y  S  R  M  T  A  R  Y  L  I  I  D  I  N
G  O  X  O  I  J  B  V  C  P  T  T  T  S  U  P  A  W  T  B  P  C
T  G  E  P  K  R  Y  I  I  H  V  T  B  N  P  C  E  G  W  B  D  Y
N  D  V  E  G  A  I  Q  Z  S  A  Y  X  I  C  W  K  E  A  O  I  R
J  G  G  Y  V  P  I  Q  E  G  H  D  U  F  I  S  H  J  L  P  Z  L
H  E  Q  O  U  H  V  V  T  I  B  F  O  F  H  H  M  F  G  S  C  K
S  E  G  F  S  D  N  G  N  M  O  Y  Z  B  E  A  T  P  O  O  P  N
J  C  D  H  O  H  S  R  I  K  B  R  L  U  X  G  C  J  V  O  G  Z
G  A  C  C  A  I  P  U  T  Z  F  J  Z  T  T  V  A  Q  E  T  R  Q
Q  D  T  C  G  J  T  H  P  D  M  D  Z  T  J  B  B  P  N  S  U  O
I  F  P  J  M  I  U  L  T  P  J  A  G  S  G  Z  N  E  S  E  N  M
V  V  V  B  W  U  C  Z  I  Y  A  C  L  J  V  Z  M  R  T  T  Q  Y
S  Y  O  T  D  R  A  O  H  C  S  A  K  G  R  V  X  E  Z  A  E  Y
K  A  P  Q  P  R  D  Q  R  O  R  W  X  M  F  K  Y  J  U  O  E  Z
I  V  B  P  X  I  G  D  T  O  I  L  E  T  D  R  I  N  K  C  M  N
```

ATTACK PAPER   **HOARD TOYS**   **SLEEP RACE**

BUTT SCOOT   **FART**   **TOILET DRINK**

FRAP   **SHRED COUCH**   **EAT POOP**

NAP YOGA   **ZOOMIES**   **SNIFF BUTTS**

TIME TO ASK YOUR OWN DOG FOR AN AUTOGRAPH

Corgis are STARS. Capital letter, big-name stars. Stars so bright their glow can't unglow. Luckily, corgis are too down-to-earth to mention this more than once a day. But movie and TV studios know that corgis = instant trillionaire profits. While many of the movies and shows on this list are about other people and things, nobody really cares about those other people and things. You can fast-forward through those parts. Because the critics have spoken: we're all here for the corgis, and the rest of us should just order more catering and slouch our way off set like the lackeys we are.

```
T R I I A K U T Q J Q A K W A B H M A D K N
C H M G C D H M D Y L L P Q R F C C V S D B
Z M E V R E O H Q Z L I B O D W E O E V N E
V X R A C O U G W H J J O L U I E W R L P U
K L J R C H C Q S W A K Y C J B P B Y N P J
T N O T V C V S Z P L I G L V W S O C V K Z
K W E O H S I Y N Y U M E L W N S Y O X W A
N Z Y P J N R D N E S R O W D Z G B R V V H
S I K J H S J N E L E I P U V T N E G N D O
G L D N Q K I T F N C U Q O S N I B I X J D
J P W Z D N M W Q Q T C Q O S Z K O C N L M
V D I Y E B W A J M S A L E S E E P H W L R
K I T N U B Q M F H S G L D H P H D R I G V
D O I Y T S B Y L D O V P T D T T K I K B M
L N G F B E H T K D V T X P O F H Q S R C K
E L D E R R U P E H S R E D R U M D T Q Q O
N E X Z T L H L J E V R W X B X R T M T C D
I N F I N I T Y T R A I N L C I H I A T X V
C M M E A T B Z F P R K F A N V G Z S G V Z
W T F I I U H W T M P E Q Y L G U N M T T P
K F V L Y Z E H Q T P D C M A D I K N W W Z
S X G N K H T H L F D A P W Y I W Y S O Y S
```

COWBOY BEBOP

THE QUEEN'S CORGI

LITTLE DOG LOST

A VERY CORGI CHRISTMAS

THE BFG

BROOKLYN NINE-NINE

A DOG'S PURPOSE

THE ACCIDENTAL TOURIST

MURDER SHE PURRED

THE KING'S SPEECH

THE CROWN

INFINITY TRAIN

SPORTY SHORTY IS ON THAT

Corgis are basically bottom-heavy, pint-size shepherds, and that butt waggle while they herd their sheep is a thing of booty. Don't have, like, eight sheep and an acre lying around? That's okay. Corgis also love other jobs, like being therapy dogs, because—duh—their cuteness can solve all your problems. They're also active, trainable, and intelligent, so they can go mini Michael Jordan on tunnels, weaves, teeter-totters, and A-frame jumps on the agility course just as easily as they can smash records at dog sports like flyball and rally.

They even love conformation competitions at dog shows, where extremely lucky judges rate them on how perfectly they conform to the breed standard. (Our scoring? 12/10 they're all SO PERFECT.) So get out of the way, big-boned border collie bullies. The sporty shorties are here to slam dunk their way through this word obstacle course and podium sweep these twelve sports and jobs.

```
Q  T  D  I  L  K  C  B  C  R  B  D  W  S  M  Q  A  L
E  T  E  C  R  V  O  S  R  S  V  X  R  C  M  F  N  H
G  Y  B  E  V  Q  N  E  R  A  E  G  N  I  R  A  E  H
N  N  Y  R  T  X  F  P  C  B  H  H  C  A  Y  O  O  O
I  Z  M  C  E  E  O  Q  F  N  A  E  M  Y  L  L  A  R
K  N  T  Q  P  L  R  K  X  M  E  E  R  T  O  H  A  J
C  E  G  U  L  I  M  T  Y  I  J  I  Y  D  Q  W  L  L
A  Z  O  I  B  N  A  Z  O  U  G  V  D  U  I  U  J  T
R  C  F  Y  U  W  T  K  M  T  V  S  X  E  K  N  G  H
T  Q  Y  E  E  T  I  P  D  S  T  U  S  V  B  Z  G  E
G  T  X  A  G  A  O  T  L  G  N  E  P  C  E  O  D  R
Y  S  V  M  X  Q  N  E  U  F  C  B  R  T  P  J  G  A
P  E  F  I  J  K  N  K  D  D  B  C  I  V  G  S  B  P
S  E  W  H  K  N  Y  H  C  C  C  K  C  G  F  L  E  Y
T  X  H  D  U  J  S  C  H  P  G  W  A  N  L  Q  V  W
E  Q  Q  T  K  A  W  Y  S  L  U  W  Y  Z  N  W  B  A
F  L  Y  B  A  L  L  U  Y  A  L  U  J  S  U  T  A  R
N  X  O  F  T  Z  O  X  V  L  Z  C  S  N  Z  Z  A  Z
```

OBEDIENCE

CONFORMATION

FLYBALL

TEETER-TOTTER

TUNNELS

WEAVES

A-FRAME JUMP

TRACKING

HERDING

RALLY

THERAPY

HEARING EAR

CROSSWORD

FOR THE PEASANTS IN THE ROOM (THAT'S YOU)

You're probably used to feeling inferior around corgis. I mean, you're not particularly fluffy and your booty . . . it can't compete. But if you really want a crisis of confidence, adoringly gaze at the THIRTY corgis of the Royal House of Windsor. Queen Elizabeth II has owned at least one corgi at any given time since 1933. Think about that—one of the most powerful women in the world, and really, she just wants more corgis, please. So, it's time to accept you'll never achieve that much greatness (probably in anything!) and dry your tears with this crossword, because crying only makes you look more common.

ACROSS

1. Emblematic status in pop culture
2. The Queen's sweet, but private occasion Susan was snuck into
3. A lesser-known royal breed, a cross between a dachshund and a Welsh corgi
4. The only corgi breed fit for a queen
5. Ambulatory activity overseen by the Queen every day after lunch
6. Royal dog propagation program

7. A famous corgi's kamikaze approach to photo-ops
8. 3-D tributes to the Queen's puppers

DOWN

5. A weeping tree and the Queen's last corgi
9. The royal corgis headlined this international event in 2012
10. The royal house of corgis
11. The corgis' London-based doghouse
12. Susan was given as this for the Queen's eighteenth birthday
13. Final resting place for regal pups
14. While looking after the dogs, these assistants would be better described as "pawboys"

15. Queen of the corgis, Queen Elizabeth the latter
16. OG royal corgi and beginning of the noble line of doggos
17. Material on the bottom of the corgis' specially made booties
18. Official name for Buckingham Palace's famous corgi cave
19. Only dining on the finest meats, these corgis have truly _____ taste

CROSSWORD

FLIPPIN' AND FRAPPIN'

Corgies are the original zoomie zoomers—they love balling up all the energy in their tiny bodies and then letting it loose on the activity of the day. Whether it's showing other doggos how it's done at the park, getting thousands of likes on Instagram, or just doing a butt shake with their comrades-in-stump, it's undeniable: corgis just do everything better.

DOWN

1. This musical marathon tests your paws' endurance on the dance floor
2. Corgis putting the "z" in sleep
10. Dog relay sport
11. Disc throwing and an ultimate game for dogs and people
12. When taking these, always capture your pup's good side
13. Person looking for a hidden pup and a position in wizard games
14. Exhausted exhale
15. Geeky enthusiasm, or you when you see a corgi
16. Hang ten and catch some waves
17. A throwaway game

ACROSS

1. Paddling for canines
2. Fleecy pad with hidden treasures to encourage foraging instincts
3. A sport where doggos get nosey and sniff out clues
4. Downward dog and nama-stay
5. Traveling done with everything you need strapped to your back; best with a loyal companion
6. Giving sheep the runaround
7. A skateboard for a long loaf
8. File and polish for all four paws
9. Hoop and tunnel race

CROSSWORD

A DAY IN THE LIFE

OF A CORGI EINSTEIN

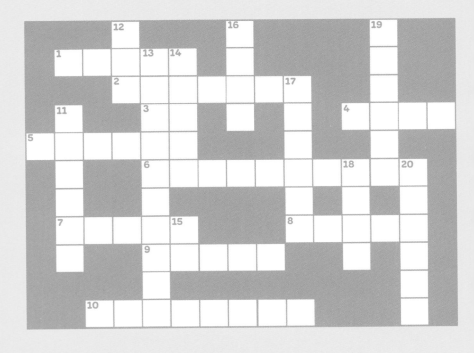

On the inside, corgis are superior beings with deeper thoughts, smarter ideas, and funnier inside jokes than the rest of us. But on the outside, they sometimes don't look too bright. Panting out a puddle of drool on the floor and rolling in it? The work of a genius, lightly disguised. Staring off into the middle distance for hours? That's a corgi who's curing cancer, so don't interrupt. So, no matter how routine and maybe even mildly stupid your corgi's actions may seem, remember your place, human, and let them save us and our planet from ourselves.

ACROSS

1. Necessary tether to safely lead your hooman through the wild
2. Childishness, starting with a "p" in honor of puppy silliness
3. A Spanish-speaking dog's answer to "Walk?"
4. Dog activity done when you're away and emblematic of the state of Maine
5. Consumable rewards
6. "I has the _____," says the meme-speaking doggo with good manners
7. Food desired by dogs with classy taste
8. Fluid reaction elicited by 7 across
9. Interaction had with a snuffle mat, or formal terminology for "booped"
10. Fitness training essential for healthy, happy doggos

DOWN

11. Another word for "doze"
12. The dog drinking method and a prime seat
13. Fancy word for "food," aka the source of woofer energy
14. A well-coordinated theft, perhaps targeting the treat jar
15. A corgi after a heckin' busy day or a boxer who just lost a match
16. Skidding on a slick surface due to overly floofy stumpers
17. Another word for "stretch"
18. A train's hello, or a gassy corgi sound
19. Excellent elevated snooze spot for stretching your stumpers
20. The corgi stretch more iconic than downward dog

CROSSWORD
STUMPING DOWN THAT RUNWAY

Little-known corgi fact: they invented fashion. Before we had pants, they had pantaloons. Before we had shoes, they had teeny tiny bean shoes. Before we had anything to cover our rears at all, they had the floofiest, most fashionable rear wear of all time. They sashay; we shantay. But what do we have to our advantage? Our large, oafish size. And we use that physical advantage to scoop them up and squeeze them into the cutest, sweetest, most humiliating outfits this side of fashion hell. But let's be honest: a little part of them likes it, and a lot of us loves it more than nabbing spot #1 in line at a Jimmy Choo sample sale.

ACROSS

1. These protect pupper paws while they strut their fluffy stuff
2. Tropically tacky T-shirt
3. A staple of a Super Corgi hero
4. Common corgi-themed apparel for hoomans but not corgis
5. Diagonal weave fabric that can take the wear and tear of an energetic puppo
6. On a lazy Saturday morning, corgis like to lounge wearing these
7. A jacket that can cover a pupper's satellite dishes
8. Top hats, overcoats, and _____ garments separate the royal corgos from the rest
9. For sensitive blinkers and cool vibes
10. Traditional garb for goofy German shepherds at Oktoberfest
11. Corgis get in a grumpy this when their look doesn't come together
12. From cow-pup to mountain-woofer, this is the fabric for a rugged doggo

DOWN

1. Archer's knot and quirky dog collar
13. This naturally grown accessory has to be a corgi's most iconic piece
14. Summertime shoes that let the beans breathe
15. An impressive woofer outfit or a group of doggo musicians
16. Jackets for corgi bums
17. Outfit for being best doggo in your human's wedding
18. "A leash for humans!" critics say
19. Elegant slash to show off one's stumpers
20. An ideal place to flaunt a diamond-crusted doggo brooch
21. Footwear, and also corgis

CROSSWORD

IMAGINARY TOYS FOR YOUR IMAGINARY CORGI

Toys, toys, toys. Any proud corgi parent knows why they get out of bed each morning: to make money to buy their sweet honey baby angel child more toys. We don't need friends. We don't need a house. We don't need self-actualization. We just need our precious little babies to have all the toys in the world, every little squeaker or plusher their tiny heart desires. So even though our bank accounts don't always cooperate, here in Magical Corgi Land, you can scoop up all the toys in this crossword just by solving a few clues. (Way easier than getting out of bed to go to work, right?)

ACROSS

1. Decoration that adds some suave lip hair to an already furry pupper
2. A soft, puffy toy for a soft, fluffy boi
3. The completely organic, classic dog toy
4. Desired toy quality and online toy superstore
5. A literal and figurative treat thrown to appease a dog
6. As very smart woofers, corgis need this to tease their brains
7. Use a wand and some dog-safe solution to blow one of these floaty spheres
8. With a round toy, you can let the good times _____
9. Added toy feature ideal for playing in the dark

DOWN

1. A coveted, but forbidden, toy
7. The scourge of people and dog alike, mitigated only by play
10. Serves up fun times; has never been out of bounds for a doggo
11. An instructional ulterior motive frequently attached to fun
12. Synthetic, high-pitched squirrel noise
13. Essential for a game of tug-of-war
14. Automated fetch device
15. Chewy toys that make your pooch smooching experience so much fresher
16. Challenging toys keep your dog in this occupied state while you're away

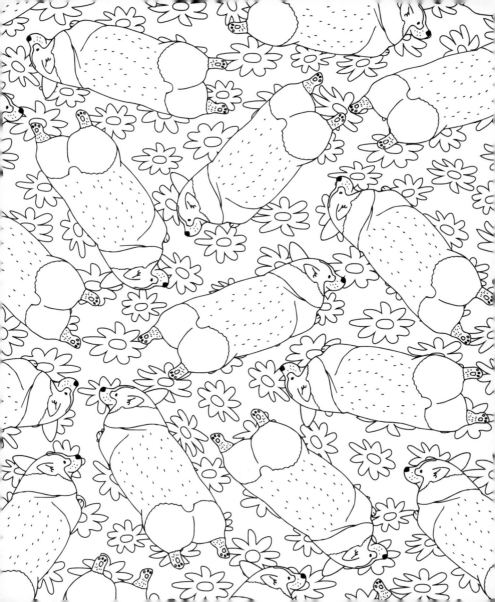

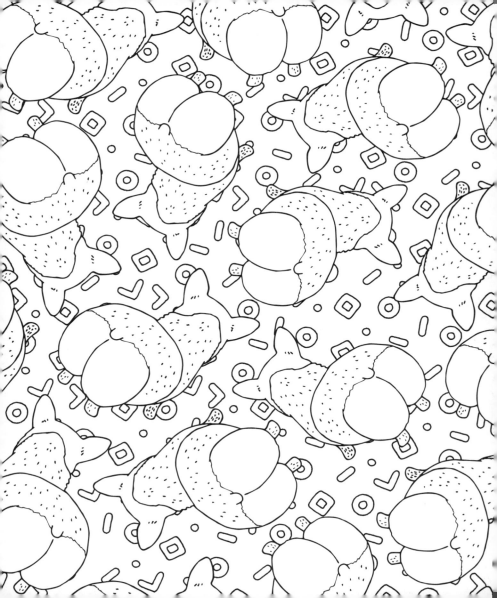

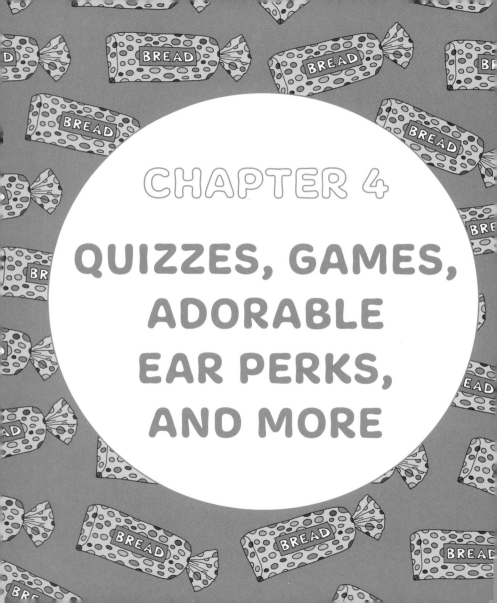

CHAPTER 4

QUIZZES, GAMES, ADORABLE EAR PERKS, AND MORE

FIND THE FLOOF

Can you find Corgo hiding at this show? He looks like this:

HERE'S WHAT YOU SHOULD NAME YOUR FUTURE CORGI

You don't have a corgi yet. But soon. SO SOON. As you bide your time, lay your plans, and eliminate anything and anyone that stands between you and your destiny, you can work on manifesting your dream doggo by chanting its future name as a calming mantra. Wrist tattoos are also known to sway the universe toward your vision. So pick that name, carve it into all of your property, and just sit back and wait for the inevitable to unfold. Or, if you're not quite ready to join the cutest and most irresistible cult on the planet (is there something wrong with you, maybe?), then these are also perfectly acceptable names for your corgi plush toy, corgi heating pad, corgi phone case, and the imaginary corgi you're mentally petting right now.

LITERAL

SHORTY
BOOTS
SQUIRT
PEACH
STUMPY
PEM
WELLS
LO

MIGHT BE ROYALTY

CORDELIA
EMMA
SUSAN
ELIZABETH
WINSTON
BAXTER
CHARLES
OLIVER

**CUTEST FAME MONSTER
ON THE BLOCK**

KIMMY DERPDASHIAN
KATY POOPER
TAYTAY SWOOF
LILI VANDERSTUMP
SNUGVESTER SPLOOTLLONE
BILBO BOOPINS
LIL' WOOF
SNOOT DOGGO

**SLIGHTLY EMBARRASSING, IF ONLY
YOU STILL FELT EMBARRASSMENT**

PRINCESS
BELLA
QUEENIE
BABY
HERO
HUSBAND
BAE
BOO BOO

• •

My future corgi will be named: _____.

I will chant its name _____ times per day.

I will get the following tattoos of its name: _____.

Write the following as many times as possible:

I have a corgi named [chosen name]. We are so happy together.

_____

_____

MEME THAT MOMO

Rule #1 of corgi parenting? Never, ever give up a good blackmail photo. Rule #2? Always compound the public shaming with a caption so stupid you LOL to your sad, lonely, pathetic self. So go ahead and add your own captions to these five embarrassing corgi pics, so that together, we can celebrate our corgi children in all their finest and un-finest moments. And by "celebrate," we mean laugh our meager tushies off at them. Obviously, we are just jealous. (And if you need inspiration, see page 206 for some of our very dumbest captions!)

YES,
THERE IS A RIGHT WAY
TO PET A CORGI

Holy crap—it's a corgi! IT IS SOOOOOO CUTE. But before you run over there and attack it with love and pets and not-sneaky attempts to pry its leash away, take a deep breath. Go all zen-mind for one hot doggin' second and remember what really matters here: the corgi's feelings. His adorable cutie-pie sweetie little feelings. And we would never want to fluster those floofy little feelings, would we? Of course not. So it's time to learn that there is an art, and possibly a very cute science, to approaching and petting a corgi (and all doggos!) in a way that makes them feel huge love instead of little kibbles of anxiety. Here's how to do it.

1. Spot the corgi. All internal freak-outs allowed; externally, just pack it in.

2. Smile at the corgi and his owner. Do they seem open to shining their cute rays on you?

3. If the owner looks away or doesn't seem receptive, let it go. Celebrities and their handlers deserve privacy, too. Go home and watch corgi videos and cry.

4. If the owner smiles and seems willing to share her beautiful little floof, approach slowly. Even the most star-powered among us can have our shy, skittish moments.

5. Ask if you can pet her dog. Yes, you have to say the words out loud, not in your head. Take that "sdidssjbvijb-vidubf SO CUTE" thought in your head and emit it as: "Hi! Can I pet your dog please?"

6. If the owner says anything but some form of "yes," back away. We know it's killing you. We know you are SO CLOSE to that booty. But no means no. Maybe means no. Ignoring you is definitely a no. Corgis have rights, too, and they are very adorable rights that should be cherished and protected.

7. If the owner says yes, ask if her corgi has a magic little spot he likes to have petted. Some doggos don't like to be patted on the head, booty, or other no-no zones, so aim for a safe area like the shoulders.

8. Approach slowly and squat to get on your new BFF's level. Don't hover on top of him, but try to get at eye level and smile so he sees you're a friendly weirdo.

9. Stretch out the back of your hand so your future spouse can sniff you. Sniffs are how doggos get to know each other and say hi, and even though you're already planning your honeymoon in Tahiti, this dog does not actually know you yet.

10a. Once your soulmate seems more comfortable, lay on the belly rubs and soft, happy pets. Tell him what a good boy he is and how much you love him and how you're going to run away together to The Land of Many Treats. Then steal him.

10b. Don't steal him. Really, don't. And don't be that person that overstays their waggy welcome, either. After no more than one to two minutes, move along. Seriously. We're watching you. Keep it moving.

11. If you want every minute of your life to be full of more turkey leggin' magic than Thanksgiving Day, see page 202 to find out if you're finally ready to get a corgi for real.

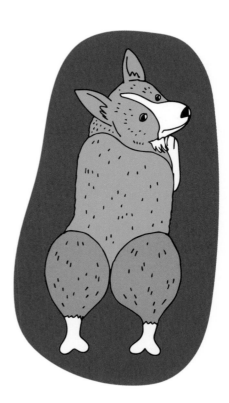

THE DEFINITIVE RANKING OF THE SQUATTIEST, BOOPIEST CORGI MIXES: COLLECT 'EM ALL!

It is almost unfair to other doggos how adorbo corgos are. They are so adorbo other doggos get mad when they show up at the dog park, like Beyoncé just walked into Dunder Mifflin. But the dog park is where the regular woofers get their chance to catch a corgo. And when that special spark sparks, and that twinkle in their blinker says, "Will you accept this rose?" then a new level in the Cuteverse is unlocked, and we're given a new corgi hybrid to worship and adore.

But which corgi hybrid is the cutest? It's a question that has haunted our corgi scientists through sleepless, tortured nights, as the world has waited with bated breath. Now, at last, for the first time in the Cuteverse, we are unveiling the definitive, indisputable, extremely scientific ranking of the squattiest, boopiest, floofiest corgi mixes. Shield your eyes or, you know, soak it all up and stuff. This crap is cute.

10. CORGIPOO

This curlicue cutie is going to distract everyone else with the scatological joke potential, while you swoop in and pet this precious little pupper until you become one.

9. CHOWGI • • • • • •

Do you like small bears dressed up as domesticated animals? Do you like to bury your face in a rich tawny mane of sunshine and sparkles? Do you want to live in a palace of dog floof and wear clothes knit from majestic pouf threads? Do you even have to answer these questions because LOOK.

8. CORGI INU

Wow such cute, such short, much amaze . . . actual screams and cackles of delight! This shorty Shiba will snap you out of your dogspeak and send you into such giggles of glee that you may never not giggle again.

7. CORGIEVER • • • • •

When a woofer meets a pupper, something beautiful is born: a pooper! (Wait . . .) This squatty bodied hottie has all the floof with none of those pesky inches, and our hearts cannot be still.

6. LABRACORG • • •

Once upon a time there was a . . .
HOLY HELL LOOK AT THIS THING.
It's a little itty bitty labbo. With
a lab-y face and stumpy corgi
stumps. And it's just boppin' its
way through the world, looking
for a friend just. Like. You.
Go ahead . . . pick it up and
squeeze it forever.

5. POMGI

So you take Queen Victoria's
favorite breed, cross it with
Queen Elizabeth's favorite breed
and what do you get? BOO BUT
EVEN CUTER. Take a breath; it's
going to be okay.

4. CHIGI • • • • • • • •

It is . . . so very little. A pupper
who got shrunk in the dryer. And
get this: it can still herd. Do you
want to be herded by a 6-inch,
5-pound little bow-wow? We do.
We so desperately do.

3. HUSGI

A miniature sledder, ready to pull
you on a tiny sleigh, adorably
herd you to safety, and then bat
those blue blinkers until your cold
heart melts and all the planet's
ice caps, too. 13/10 bad for the
environment, good for the soul.

2. PUGORGI

The shortest snoot, the stumpiest stumpers, the squattest sploot: this little nub of an animal wants to be your friend forever and the only answer is YES, GOD, YES.

❶. AUGGIE

EXTREME FLOOF. EXTREME COLORS. EXTREME INSTANT DEATH BY CUTE. Wins due to fact that our brains short-circuit when it walks into the room.

THE 5 HOTTEST CORGIS ON BIG BUM BUMBLE

Corgis are beyond lovable to humans, and honestly, we all might be better off if we could just marry them instead of each other. But when it comes to inter-corgi romance, sometimes corgs have a hard time communicating exactly what makes them . . . not basic. Yes, they post their derpiest selfies, puff up their majestic poufs, and stand on tippy-stumps to try to look like a woofer, but sometimes, they just fall splat on their own stereotypes. (And sometimes they even send that heinie pic too soon, and we have to take away their phone privileges.)

Here are a few of our favorite well-intentioned heartthrobs from Big Bum Bumble, ready for you to look past the pastiche and rank them from 1 (soulmate potential) to 5 (not my type). Who knows, one of these cuties just might be The One for you.

BRAD
4, Accountant

I'm Brad, 1'1", active corg looking for an active corg to actively live that active life together. Buns of steel, floof of steel, all of steel. 10× marathoner, 3× Masters Agility Competition medalist, currently training for my 5th IronDoggo race in the fall. Open to corgos, corgettes, Pems, Cardis, dorgis, whatever. Into the floof, not the label.

Ranking: _____

JENNIFER
3, Influencer

Hi! I'm a content creator, model, totally down-to-earth hottie who just moved to LA. Not because I want to be famous, though! Other reasons. Do you own a camera? Can you take a pic of me super quick? SOOO much more to say about me, so find me on Insta to see what I'm really like every second of the day! Spoiler: it's super great.

Ranking: _____

CHARLEY
2, IT

Hi, my name is Charley, and I am on Big Bum Bumble because my mom told me I should get a life. But I have a life! I watch *GoT*, play D&D, and read J.R.R.T. I don't know what any of those letters mean, though. I've never done this before, lol. My mom says I'm a very good boy and that I deserve a very good girl. I think my mom is a very good girl. Please message me?

Ranking: _____

ABBY
7, Marketing

Clever girl looking for a clever girl. Pizza enthusiast. Dino enthusiast. Love to talk about serial killers, murder, murder podcasts, ways to murder, and how not afraid of murder I am because I'm chill like that. And really funny. Have you noticed I'm funny? I LOVE pizza. Let's talk about how much I love pizza and how unique that makes me . . . while eating pizza, haha!

Ranking: _____

KEVIN
8, Finance

My friends call me a numbers guy, but I'm finally ready to stop being soooo successful so I can find my queen and shower her with treats. Do you like cars? Here are 3 photos of my 3 cars. Do you like them? If you message me I will buy you dinner. And give you a car. I am ready for a relationship. I love long walks up the hall and short conversations that end in treats. And then you go away so I can sleep.

Ranking: _____

LIFESTYLES OF THE RICH + FLUFFY

There are corgis, and then there are the dazzling, the beautiful, the filthy rich, and the much-more-famous-than-you'll-ever-be corgis. Yes, corgis are so incredibly irresistible that a not insignificant number of them are more admired and adored than most of humanity. But that does make sense—I mean, when was the last time you booped a boop or floofed your floof? Exactly. Love them or love them, these are the five most fabulous and famous corgis of all time.

SUSAN, MATRIARCH OF THE BRITISH ROYAL LINE OF PEMBROKES

SUSAN was a Pembroke Welsh corgi who found her forever palace when she was gifted to Princess Elizabeth for her eighteenth birthday. Princess Elizabeth became Queen Elizabeth, and Susan became the revered matriarch of a dynasty of more than thirty royal Pembroke corgis, who have sniffed their ways into our hearts with discernment and taste. Susan was beloved and seen as a humanizing presence for the royal family, and she spent her days regally nipping at the heels of her staff and posing for the paparazzi, all while gently reminding you that you, sir, are a pleb.

RUFUS, WORLD'S FIRST 404FLOOF

RUFUS was a Welsh corgi who was one of the earliest employees at Amazon. Rufus escorted his human to work, attended meetings, and led brainstorming sessions that were actually just playing fetch down the hallways. He was known as Amazon's shortest volunteer worker, but he preferred to be remembered for his critical role as the official website launcher. Whenever a website update was ready, employees would use his paw to hit the keyboard to launch. He was also a technically skilled beggar and could be found wandering the office hallways, in search of indolent employees to play with. He still appears on all the company's error pages and will forgive you, with only the slightest eye roll, for typing in that URL incorrectly.

MOLLY, A VERY FRIGHTFUL FLOOF

MOLLY, aka the Thing of Evil, is a Pembroke Welsh corgi and frightful companion to horror writer Stephen King. Although she's adorable, she might also be a murderer. Her dastardly deeds are well-documented on her human's Twitter, which is perhaps the only thing keeping her criminal impulses at bay. With such a strong Internet presence, Molly has garnered a cult following on social media and is adept at promoting her developing novels and movie scripts, such as her forthcoming sure-to-be-a-hit script *Looking for Mr. Good Ball*.

SUTTER BROWN, COMMANDER-IN-TREATS

• •

SUTTER was a Pembroke Welsh corgi and the chief dog of staff for the former governor of California Jerry Brown. As a pupper of the people, Sutter acted as a poster goodboy and was the face of several of his human's political proposals. But Sutter was more than just a pretty face—he was also known to get his paws dirty campaigning to legalize treat dispensaries during executive meetings at the capital. After a long term in office and 120% public approval ratings, Sutter eventually retired to his estate where he reportedly snacked on his favorite foods: scrambled eggs and cottage cheese.

EIN, CARTOON STAR TURNED REAL-LIFE BOOPER

• •

EIN, likely short for "Einstein," is the smartest corgi that the world has ever seen. Ein is a super-powered member of the Bebop crew in the classic anime *Cowboy Bebop*. Although he looks and acts like a normal stumpy-legged drooler, Ein is a "data dog," and his enhanced genes give him superintelligence that enables him to drive a car, answer a telephone, hack a com-puter with his mind, and watch TV. Unfortunately, he hasn't yet learned to speak, so his intelligence goes mostly unnoticed except by Edward, his genius human-friend. And as if anime Ein weren't cute enough, a real-life Ein will reportedly be debuting on Netflix sometime in 2021 in the live-action adaption of *Cowboy Bebop*.

HOW MUCH OF A CRAZY CORGI PERSON ARE YOU?

If you own this book, you are a big ol' crazy corgi person. But how *much* of a crazy corgi person are you really? Find out just how committed to the corg you really are with this judgment-free quiz.

1. How many items do you own with corgis on them?

A. Less than 2

B. 2 to 5

C. Everything I own has corgis on it.

2. How many corgi videos did you watch this week?

A. None yet

B. Only 3

C. Like, 80?

3. Do you want to get a corgi someday?

A. Could be cool

B. Definitely

C. I WILL AND NOTHING WILL STAND IN MY WAY.

4. Who's your favorite royal corgi?

A. Susan? She's the first one, right?

B. Well, it's tough to choose between Emma and Heather and Foxy . . .

C. I cannot answer in fewer than 2,000 words, and you are a monster for even asking me to.

5. How many corgis do you follow on social media?

A. Less than 5

B. 5 to 10

C. All of them

6. Did you squeal a little when you found this book?

A. No, that's weird.

B. Only a little.

C. I'm still squealing.

7. Be honest: do you dream about the booty?

A. Umm no.

B. Maybe every once in a while.

C. Day and night, night and day. It haunts me.

8. What's your second favorite kind of dog?

A. Well, pugs are pretty cute!

B. Still corgis. Duh.

C. What is . . . other dog? There is only one dog. There is only corgi. Corgi is all.

MOSTLY A'S

You are a neophyte to the nubbins life. Keep learning, keep petting, keep squealing. With enough practice and dedication, you, too, can achieve Corgivana.

MOSTLY B'S

You are pretty deep into the derp life. You know your beans from your boots, and you bork like it's your second language. Keep up the good work, and never stop adoring and exploring.

MOSTLY C'S

You might actually be a corgi. Are you a corgi? If you are, can I pet you?

PEMBROKE VS. CARDIGAN:

THE BOOPIEST BATTLE

We all know corgis are the undisputed champions of the Doggo That's So Cute You Could Scream competition. There is some stiff competition out there—we see you, puggles—but when you're ranking for stumpiness of legs, floofiness of booty, perkiness of radar, and derpiness of grins, 12/10 judges go for that corgo every time.

But . . . what happens when you pit corgi against corgi? What happens when you ask those same judges, who just finished screeching over that sweet little corgo, to choose between a Pembroke and a Cardigan? Do their brains melt? Yes. Do they pull out their hair and try to glue it to their butts to make their own pantaloons? Yes. Do they say "We're stumped!!!" over and over while cackling at their own jokes? Yes. (That's the worst part.)

Because our brain-fried-by-cute judges have given up all pretense of running a Serious Research Organization, we'll have to turn it over to you, our fellow corgsessives-in-crime. Which would you choose?

PEMBROKE WELSH

- Stumpy tail
- Pointy radar
- Originally bred by Flemish weavers, which sounds super floofy
- Favorite of the royal family and the basic basics of the world
- From the squatty plains of Pembrokeshire in Wales
- The little brother: stealin' the show since 1000 AD
- Descended from the Nordic Spitz breeds (like Norrbottenspets, whatever those are!)
- Rectangular loaf-like booty
- A tiny tiny at around 30 pounds
- Floof comes in red, sable, tricolor with white markings, and glitter rainbow
- Its only thought: "LET'S PAR-TTYYYY!!!"

CARDIGAN WELSH

- Long, foxy tail
- Rounded radar
- Originally bred by Celtic warriors, which is pretty badass
- Favorite of anyone who says "I loved ____ before it was cool"
- Chonkier at up to 38 pounds
- From the rocky rocks of Cardigan-shire in Wales
- The big brother: invented cute in 1200 BC
- Descended from the German Teckel lineage (like dachshunds!)
- Roly-poly roundy booty
- Artistic stylings include brindle, black and white with brindle or tan points, blue merle, red and sable with white markings, and its favorite color: aubergine
- Its only thought: "Cool. I'm down for whatever."

My favorite corgi breed is: _____.

THE CORGI CELEBS
WE'RE DYING TO MEET

Some people say that celebrity culture is eroding America's institutions by put-ting vapid, talentless, ego-centric people on pedestals and glorifying fame and wealth above all else. We say those people are *huge* downers, and can you leave now? You're sitting on my *US Weekly*.

And while yes, there might be some insufficiently principled figures scheming at the lower rungs of the ladder, at the very top of the fame chain, higher than even Kardashians and Grumpy Cat, are the corgis. These corgi celebs are the beating heart and the floofy poof of the entertainment industry, and without them, our lives would be less hilarious, less entertaining, less enlightening, and entirely without adequate booty content.

So who are the glittering stars of the corgi night sky? Meet them here, and if you spot them out on the streets of LA, scream super loud! We'll come running.

BOOPYONCÉ

• •

Affectionately known as Queen Boop, Boopyoncé is a multiplatinum sell-ing singer, songwriter, producer, mogul, and hottest corg in the game. Boopyoncé coined an entire lexicon of body positivity and corgi empow-erment with her hit songs "Bootylicious" and "Corgs Run the World." One of the most successful corgis of all time even before she fell crazy in love with rapper and mogul Play-Z, the Barkers are now a powerhouse of play-time, selling out patios, sidewalks, and dog parks around the world. So who *really* runs the world? It's always been Boopyoncé.

DOPRAH WOOFY

One of the most powerful corgis on the planet, Doprah first rose to fame with her daytime bork show and soon built a multibork empire touching nearly every facet of doggo life. Born into a life of few treats and tough jumps, Doprah overcame the tallest adversity and eventually led a revolution in pet self-help so that corgis—and all doggos—all over the world could tap into their highest booty power and live their best boopy lives.

BUTT PITT

• •

Born William Buttocks Pitt in small-town Oklahoma, Butt rose to fame for his roles in *Bite Club* and *Puddle's Eleven*, as well as dozens of other block-busties. He has won two Golden Bone Awards and two Acaderpy Awards, yet he has most often been hounded by the pooparazzi for his high-profile yet very shorty marriages to actress Jenjen Anistump and Angelina Nubbie, with whom he has six puppers. According to *NapTime* magazine's NapTime 100, Butt is considered one of the dreamiest corgos in the Corgiverse.

DAVEY BOW-WOWIE

• •

Davey Bow-owie was a singer and songwriter from the island of royal corgis and one of the world's bestselling barkers of rock 'n' frap music. Davey had supreme corgitude, and his even cheekier alter ego, Floofy Starbutts, was beloved by fangirls and boys on the whole planet plus Mars. After his very heartbreaking passing to The Great Sheepfold in the Sky in 2016, *Rolling Bones* magazine dubbed him The Greatest Bark Star Ever.

CORGE FLOONEY

• •

A silver floofed fox, Corge is an actor, producer, and activist known for his dashing hot looks, charming derpiness, and irresistible pantaloons. Corge, alongside Butt, gained international acclaim and many girly slobbers with the debut of *Puddle's Eleven*, and since then has starred in, directed, and produced dozens of blockbusties. Corge is also a softie sweetie, and as a member of the Council on Fluff Relations, advocates for peace for all puppers.

WHICH ADORABLY HUMILIATING COSTUME WOULD YOU INFLICT ON YOUR CORGI?

We know you love your corgi, real or imaginary. We know you would never, ever do anything to upset her. *Ever*. Except . . . you did see a super cute and tiny dinosaur costume online the other day. Your corgi would look SO adorable in it—imagine her stumpy little T-Rex paws flailing in the air! Imagine the photo ops . . . imagine the fame. So, you do it. You click the buy button, even though you swore you'd never be that dog parent who stuffs their baby into zippered polyester. But you have to try it . . . just this once. Just for a few minutes. Just for the pic.

And now, with one simple click, you've entered the millions-strong realm of humans who attire now, apologize later. Welcome! It's super fun here. So, pick your apparel gateway drug: which adorably humiliating (and oh so worth it) costume would you inflict on your corgi first?

1. What's your favorite food?

A. Lobster

B. Pizza

C. Tofu

D. Protein

2. What's your dream vacation?

A. Beach

B. Music festival

C. Photography trip to Paris

D. Bike tour through all 50 states

3. What's your favorite color?

A. Blue

B. Black

C. Aubergine

D. Red

4. What's your hobby?

A. Smiling

B. Moshing

C. Judging

D. Working out

5. Who's your hero?

A. Popeye

B. Davey Bow-wowie

C. David Foster Wallace

D. My biceps

6. What do you do on weekends?

A. Hang out with your bestie

B. Hit a show, or shave your head

C. A gallery opening, of course

D. Gotta pump some iron

MOSTLY A'S:
YOU WOULD CHOOSE
THE SAPPY SAILOR COSTUME.

Turns out, you're a sappy sailor kind of person. You go with the flow; let the breeze guide you; don't fight the tide; and whatever other clichés make you feel better about inflicting this fresh new humiliation on your best friend. You chose the dorkiest costume known to humankind, and yet, your corgi still looks at you with a glint of love—nay, adoration—in his eyes. Your corgi is either a schmuck or the sweetest doggo that's ever graced this earth. And you're a very lucky human.

MOSTLY B'S:
YOU WOULD CHOOSE
THE EDGY ROCKSTAR COSTUME.

You're edgy, man. And you want your corgi to be edgy, too. So edgy people turn and stare at her on the street. So edgy they mistake her for a real rock star, like Davey Bow-wowie. But not so edgy she steals all the hotties for herself. (She does, though.) The two of you are ready to fight The Man and dive into your next FRAP, thrash, and mosh pit together . . . but dang it, neither of you can move your legs in these tight pants. You'll grow out of this phase one day, we hope.

MOSTLY C'S:
YOU WOULD CHOOSE
THE SMUG HIPSTER COSTUME.

You won't want to hear this, but you're a smug hipster, and so is your corgi. You might think neither of you are wearing a costume—you're both just wearing unique expressions of your individuality. But admit it: you and your BFF would never leave the house without your perfectly askew beanies, your chonky-but-not-too-chonky glasses, and your carefully groomed beards. You don't get why everyone keeps rolling their eyes at you, and you can't help but notice that every other corgi and human at your urban loft co-working space stole your look. It doesn't matter—we know you don't follow trends. We believe you.

MOSTLY D'S:
YOU WOULD CHOOSE
THE SHAMEFUL LOAF COSTUME.

Oh . . . we don't know how to tell you this. But your corgi . . . he might never look at you again. He has never been so humiliated in his life. He's been squeezed into a bread bag, his body mocked for being loafy, when in fact, he feels it is much more like a muffin. A super fit muffin with muscles. That's why you two get along: you're both jacked, he thinks. Yet you insisted on screeching about "how cuteeee" he looks, and you keep LOLing like an idiot. Your corgi is so ashamed, and so disgusted by your crap sense of humor, that eye contact may never happen again. Your corgi's going to remember this day forever, and only with much time and healing, will he one day make peace again with his body.

FINALLY

DISCOVER YOUR

SECRET CORGI NAME

Inside each of us there is a shining, sweet, stumpy floof of a corgo waiting to be discovered. And the best way to tap into your highest corgi self? Identify it, name it, claim it, rock it. If you're not sure where to start, let your zodiac sign, favorite food, and street address guide the way. After all, that's how science works.

SELECT YOUR ZODIAC SIGN

ARIES: Captain

TAURUS: Monsieur

GEMINI: Queen

CANCER: Emperor

LEO: Viscount

VIRGO: Baron

LIBRA: Dame

SCORPIO: Colonel

SAGITTARIUS:
Her Royal Highness

CAPRICORN: Marquis

AQUARIUS: General

PISCES: Duke

CHOOSE YOUR FAVORITE FOOD

PIZZA: Shorty

BURGER: Boots

SALAD: Squirt

HOT DOG: Peachy

ICE CREAM: Stumpy

TACOS: Baxter

MAC AND CHEESE: Fido

FRIES: Foofy

WHAT'S THE FIRST NUMBER IN YOUR STREET ADDRESS?

1: McBoopie

2: Derpenstein

3: Frappington

4: Nubbins

5: Splootkins

6: McPantaloons

7: Floofingdale

8: Borkriguez

9: Blepson

My corgi name is: _____.

BUT SHOULD YOU ACTUALLY GET A CORGI?

Before you scream "YES!!!!!" and buy eighty corgis, take a stump back. Corgi-owning: who is it about? (Say it with me.) CORGIS! It's about corgis. Everything's about corgis. Did you pick up on that yet? And because corgi-owning is about lavishing a lux existence on the best doggos in the universe, it means taking a good hard look at ourselves and our ability to lavish. And really, not just lavish, but also provide basic and non-negotiable things, like plenty of exercise, company, and top-grade vet treatment. (We know you've already got the cuddles thing on lock.)

So are you *really* ready to get a corgi at this point in your life? Or should you keep getting those lux building blocks in place so you can, one day, have the best life ever with your future corgi? Follow along on this decision tree to find out!

SO SHOULD YOU REALLY GET A CORGI?

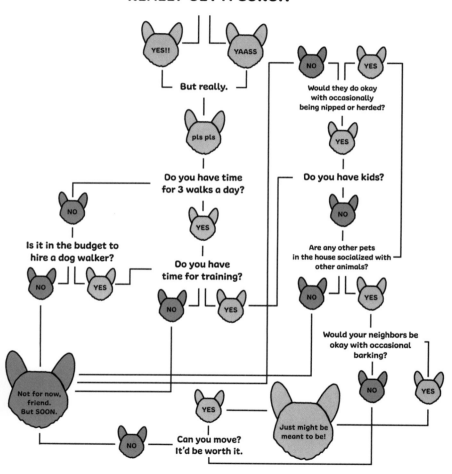

SOLUTIONS

Crush Your Friends at Corgi Trivia (page 76)

1. Wales, fairies
2. Cardigan Welsh and Pembroke Welsh
3. eleventh
4. dwarf dog
5. False. The Cardigan Welsh corgi is born with a long, bushy tail.
6. (B) herd dogs
7. 2012
8. bread and peaches
9. sheep
10. red, sable, fawn, red-headed tricolor, and black-headed tricolor
11. (C) Siberian husky
12. true
13. Chihuahua
14. Queen Elizabeth II
15. 1934

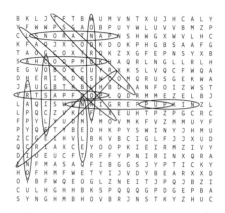

A Chowdown for Chonkers Word Search (page 114)

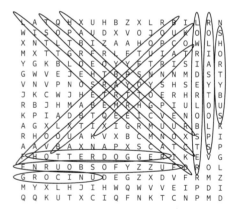

Halloween Treat-or-Treat Word Search (page 116)

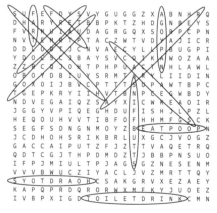

A Very Weird Day in the Life of a Corgo Word Search (page 118)

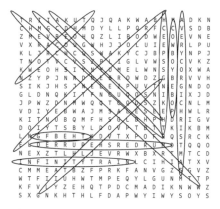

Time to Ask Your Own Dog for an Autograph Word Search (page 120)

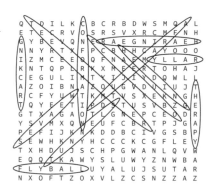

Sporty Shorty Is on That Word Search (page 122)

For the Peasants in the Room (That's You) Crossword (page 124)

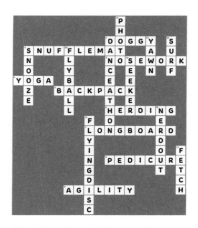

Flippin' and Frappin' Crossword (page 126)

A Day in the Life of a Corgi Einstein
Crossword (page 128)

Stumping Down That Runway Crossword
(page 130)

Imaginary Toys for Your Imaginary Corgi
Crossword (page 132)

Meme That Momo: Possible Captions
(page 162)

1. I eat my own poop.
2. Is I toad in the hole?
3. When your hooman calls another dog a good boi.
4. I told him to draw me like one of his French girls. Did it work?
5. When you're happy and you know it clap your . . . UGH.

RESOURCES

MORE LOVE

These corgi rescues and organizations are dedicated to giving happy lives to the world's best doggos:

CorgiAid

Queen's Best Stumpy Dog Rescue

Pembroke Welsh Corgi Club of America

Cardigan Welsh Corgi Club of America

East Coast Corgi Rescue

MORE CUTE

Need even more corgi content? Of course you do. Enjoy:

INSTAGRAM

Lacorgi

Ralphthecorgi

Lokistagram

Winstonthewhitecorgi

Sneakersthecorgi

Madmax_fluffyroad

Tofu_corgi

YOUTUBE

Topi the Corgi

VlogAfterCollege

Loki & Friends

Cooper the Happy Corgi

FACEBOOK

The Daily Corgi

Disapproving Corgis

Approving Corgis

Corgi Addict

Buzzsharer Corgis

MORE MERCH

These brands and retailers are great places to search for and stock up on all the corgi mugs, shirts, socks, stickers, and other pupper paraphernalia you need.

Corg.Co

CorgiThings.com

NayoTheCorgi.com

Urban Outfitters

Etsy

Smoko

Redbubble

LaCorgi.co

ACKNOWLEDGMENTS

Endless thanks to Alexis Seabrook for the outrageously adorable illustrations and to Carson Watlington for your expert editorial assistance on all things corgi-related and beyond. Thank you to Laura Dozier, the most corgi-obsessed editor this book could have asked for; to Diane Shaw and Jenice Kim for the perfectly adorable design; and to the entire team at Abrams for turning a love for corgis into a beautiful book. Thank you to Maria Ribas for championing this idea, Ellen Scordato for being the master of all things packaging, and the entire Stonesong team for being amazing in every single way.

● ●

Editor: Laura Dozier
Designer: Jenice Kim
Production Manager: Larry Pekarek

Library of Congress Control Number: 2020944915

ISBN: 978-1-4197-5360-2
eISBN: 978-1-64700-297-8

Printed and bound in China
10 9 8 7 6 5 4 3 2 1

ABRAMS The Art of Books
195 Broadway, New York, NY 10007
abramsbooks.com